EYES UP

A pictorial odyssey of life & landscape through a climber's lens

alastair lee

EYES UP

Published by Posing Productions

A pictorial odyssey of life & landscape through a climber's lens

alastair lee

08983237

Copyright © Alastair Lee 2002

ISBN 0 9541382 1 X

Published by Posing Productions. www.posingproductions.com

Eyes Up first edition 2002.

All photographs, design and graphics, text & captions by Alastair Lee.

By the same author - Oz Rock A Rock Climber's Guide to Australian Crags, Climbing New Zealand
A Crag Guide for the Travelling Rock Climber.

Printed and bound at De Montfort Press by Raithby, Lawrence & Company Limited, UK.

Acknowledgments

A special thanks goes out to the following people who've all been immensely helpful during
the production and marketing of this book. In no particular order - Jon Doran of
Outdoorsmagic.com, Adrain Berry of Planetfear.com, Steve Duffy of Aceville Press, Ken
Vickers of Cordee, Colin Matthews, Stewart Hughes, Mark Halsted, Aaron Moore, Dave Allen,
Valerie Le Clerc, Mum & Dad, Matt from Raithby Lawrence, Duncan Gray, Mark Lee, Kevin
Howett of the MC of S, Declan O'Keeffe of the MC of I, Alex Messenger of the BMC, Ian
Binnie, Oliver Drake, the unnamed Tibetans who posed so willingly, Simon Lv.

Also a mention for all those who came to my lectures in the early days - the Keswick five, the
Skipton twelve, the Sheffield nine and all the Mountaineering Clubs who took a chance by
booking my show. Thank-you whoever you are, this book would have never eventuated with-
out your encouragement for my work.

TITLE PAGE - Double exposure of an unclimbed peak in the Baimang Range, Yunnan, China.
PREVIOUS PAGE - On route for the Rob Roy Glacier, Matukituki Valley, South Island New Zealand.

CONTENTS

Colin Matthews demonstrates a 'Chimney', Toronto, Ontario, Canada.

pART I

360 degree view from the summit of the Tour Ronde 3792m, Mont Blanc Range, France.

The Dempster Highway, Yukon, Canada. On route for the Tombstone Mountains near the Arctic Circle.

Widdop Reservoir, Yorkshire, UK.

On route for the Rockies with Colin Matthews across the Canadian Prairies in Saskatchewan via the thousands of miles of the Trans-Canada Highway from Toronto in the East.

Trees by the shore of Wast Water late on a summer's evening, returning from The Napes Crag, Lake District, UK.

Deadwood from Checkamus Canyon Crag near Squamish, British Columbia, Canada.
OVERLEAF - Tibetan shepherds show their fascination in our climbing equipment, Birong Valley, Yunnan, China.

Showers at 5am as seen from Bugaboo Spire (3146m), Bugaboo Provincial Park, British Columbia, Canada.

Approaching a cloud-burst over the Rocky Mountains from the prairies
of Alberta on route for the Grassi Lakes Crag, Canada.

Alpine vista as seen from the summit of Mont Blanc du Tacul. The Grandes Jorasses is the dominant peak on the right (4208m) with the Matterhorn in Switzerland spiking the horizon to its left.

From left to right across both pages, as seen from - The Black Tusk, BC, Canada - The Rockies, Alberta, Canada - The Black Tusk, BC, Canada - Lake Te Anau Hut, New Zealand - Lake Superior, Ontario, Canada - Lake Te Anau, New Zealand - Lake Te Anue Hut, New Zealand - Charleston, West Coast, South Island, New Zealand.

Digitaly composed images - LEFT - Smoke climbs smoke from a cement factory in the Ribble Valley, Lancashire, UK. ABOVE - Climber tackles an overhanging hawthorn tree, Oxenber Scar, Yorkshire, UK.

The Castle Hill Basin, South Island, New Zealand

Bicycles on the streets of Kunming, Yunnan, China, one of several stop overs on a journey to the Himalayan fringe in Northern Yunnan.

The granite of the Cosmic Arete, as seen from the Col du Midi, Mont Blanc Range France. LEFT - Italian ridges lead to the Matterhorn in Switzerland as seen from the Tour Ronde in France. OVERLEAF - The Crown Mountain (5130m), Himalayan foothills, Northern Yunnan, China.

Two perspectives of Snowpatch Spire (3046m), Bugaboo Provincial Park, British Columbia, Canada.

360 degree panorama of the Lakeside Boulders at Widdop in Yorkshire, UK.

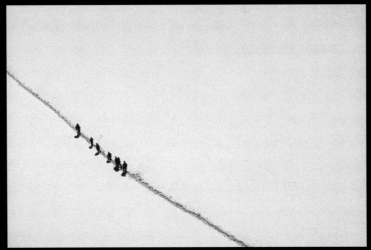

Baimang Mountain Range, Northern Yunnan, China.

As opposite, this time viewed from a mile or so across the valley.

The Kaskawulsh Glacier found in the Kluane
Nation Park in the Yukon, Canada.

LEFT - A climber's view on an easy gritstone arete at Curbar, Peak District, UK.
ABOVE - Looking down a gritstone slab at the Bridestones, Yorkshire, UK.

Lake Wanaka reflection captured on route for the sport climbing crags of Wanaka, Glendhu Bay, South Island, New Zealand.

Lyndas Pass, South Island, New Zealand.

CLOCKWISE FROM TOP LEFT - Post storm conditions as seen from the south summit of Bugaboo Spire - The east face of Bugaboo Spire - Dusk over the Canadian Rockies as seen from the south summit of Bugaboo Spire thanks to a benighting on the spire. OPPOSITE - Alpinist on the north summit of Bugaboo Spire, British Columbia, Canada.

Double exposure of complementary 5c problems on the Big Sister Boulder, Bridestones, Yorkshire, UK.

An unnamed peak (approx 5500m), Baimang Mountain Range, Northern Yunnan, China.

A dance festival at a remote village, on route for the Birong Valley, Northern Yunnan, China.

Trebble exposures, clockwise from the left - Karst towers, Yangshuo, Guangxi, China - A rock spike from Glen Coe, Scotland - The Tombstone Mountains, Yukon, Canada - Limestone towers in The Birong Valley, Northern Yunnan, China - The Old Man of Storr, Isle of Skye, Scotland.

pART II

Enjoying the expanse of the Atlantic Ocean atop the granite cliffs at Land's End in Cornwall, UK.
PREVIOUS PAGE - Alpinists on the classic beginner's route of the Petite Aiguille Verte, Mont Blanc Range, France.

The tropical waters of Lake Huron as seen from the limestone cliffs of Lion's Head, Ontario, Canada.

The 'Grand Canyon' of Europe, The Verdon Gorge, Southern France. 'Point Sublime' from three perspectives.

270 degree view of the high altitude urban expanse of Zhongdian (3300m) on the fringe of the Tibetan Plateau, Northern Yunnan, China. The final frontier before heading into the Birong & Baimang Ranges.

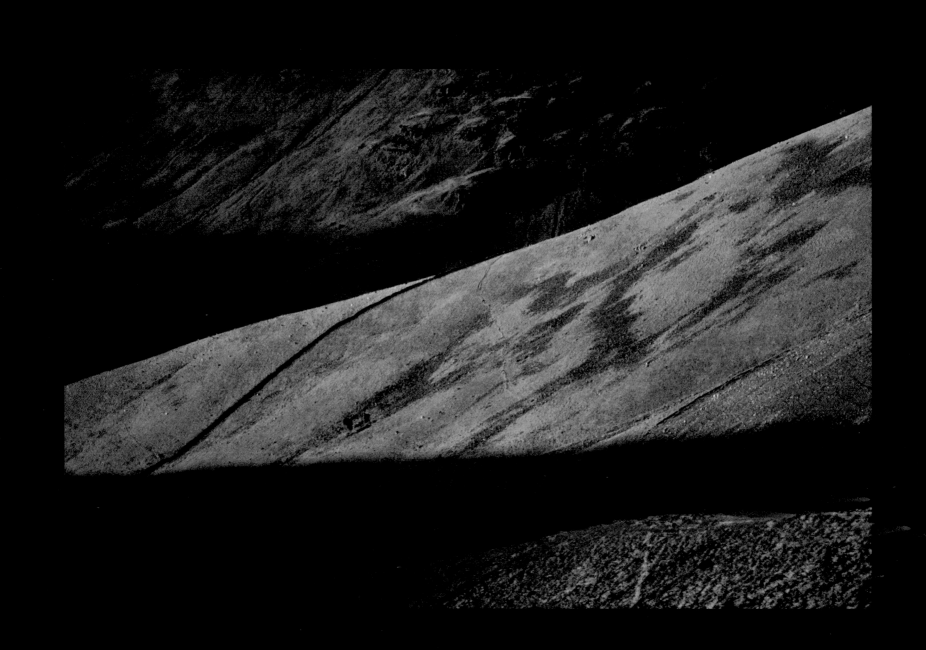

The lower reaches of Scar Fell, as seen approaching Scar Fell Crag in winter conditions, The Lake District, UK.

An inquisitive Tibetan girl and younger brother at a small village by Napa Lake near Zhongdian, Yunnan, China.

Three friends tentatively pose for the camera, Napa Lake, near Zhongdian, Yunnan, China.

A digitally composed image. Original photograph of the iris flowers was taken at Oxenber Scar, Yorkshire, UK. The climber has been cut from a 5b problem at the Lakeside Boulders, Widdop, Yorkshire, UK.

ABOVE - Valerie Le Clerc on the summit plateau of Mont Blanc du Tacul.
OPPOSITE - A serac on route for the north-west face of Mont Blanc du Tacul, Mont Blanc, France.

FROM LEFT TO RIGHT- Glacial Algae Bugaboos, BC, Canada - Ariel view of a heavily crevassed glacier, Bugaboos, BC, Canada - Lichen on the gneiss rock of NW Scotland - Snowflakes in the Cairngorms, Scotland - Rain drops on a window pane, Lancashire, UK - The Stone Forest, Yunnan, China.

FROM LEFT TO RIGHT- Dense rainforest, Vancouver Island, BC, Canada - Rain erosion on the Vowell Glacier Bugaboos, BC, Canada - Ogden Clough stream, Pendle Hill, Lancashire, UK - Fruit stall in Antalya, Turkey - Lycian inscriptions Xanthos, Turkey - Bark from the Plantation at Stanage Crag, Peak District, UK.

Two double exposures of opposing views as seen from basecamp in the Baimang Range, Northern Yunnan, China. The glacial Mt. Baimang (5600m) in one direction and the sun scorched Crown Mountain (5130m) on the other side of the valley. OVERLEAF - Maintaining finger strength with Colin Matthews on the long road to the Canadian Rockies, Trans-Canada Highway, Alberta, Canada.

The town of Punzero with its extraordinary irrigation system on the Yangtze River, Yunnan, China.

Ian Binnie on the roof climb 'Monkey Puzzle' 23 (F6c+) at Wye Creek, Lake Wakatipu, South Island, New Zealand.

Stewart Hughes tackles 'Go with the flow' 22 (F6c) on the Tenuite Wall, Sport Climbing Mecca Paynes Ford, New Zealand.
OVERLEAF - Glendhu Bay on route for the Wanaka Crags, South Island, New Zealand.

Alpinists ascend/descend the Midi Ridge, Mont Blanc, France.

The summit shadow of Mt. Taranaki (2518m), taken from the summit after a
scramble up the east ridge, North Island, New Zealand.

Sea of clouds from the 'Shark's Tooth', Mount Taranaki (2518m), New Zealand.
OVERLEAF - After nearly a week of rain, the clouds part for a display of an
unnamed peak in the Baimang Range, China.

THE
END

———————————

ABOVE - Deadwood from Checkamus Canyon Crag near Squamish, British Columbia, Canada.
PREVIOUS PAGE - Mount Taranaki at sunset, as seen from the Magetepopo Crag in the Central
North Island, New Zealand.

A note on the images

Many professional photographers have come to the realisation that over the past decade photography has been reinvented. The use of Photoshop has created new industry standards in advertising, beauty, portrait and now, landscape photography. I think this is due to both the desire to constantly improve quality and to the appeal of the new avenues Photoshop opens to the photographer. I view cameras, lenses, filters, film, tripods, technique, scanners, hardware and software with the same perspective, in that they are all tools at the disposal of the modern photographer. Reproducing the effect of a projected slide with all its range of colour, depth, detail, sharpness and contrast onto the pages of a book is no easy task. All the images in this book have been tweaked in order to represent the original slide as accurately as possible. The brilliant colours of the New Zealand and Canadian sunsets in particular really were that vivid. Its worth noting that these shots were also taken before I owned a polarising filter which of course increases contrast and colour saturation.

Although it is a sound approach to learn the theory behind a skill in order to master it. Many of the images within these pages throw the book at tradition and hope to inspire the most important factor in photography or any other artform, that of individual interpretation and expression. Concentrating too much on the law of thirds or having the very latest technology to ensure a precise exposure results in losing sight of your own ingenuity. The techniques involved in the making of EYES UP find a happy medium between traditional photographic means and contemporary digital methods, a marriage of new and old with the end result of a good image always in mind.

With the end goal being the production of a good image, the length or complexities of the procedure in realising that goal are entirely at the artist's discretion, assuming that the method is declared. Quite obviously some of the images have been digitally composed, however there are other images which have been captured by 'pure' photographic means. The double exposures of the clone climber at the Bridestones (taken on tripod and self-timer), the double exposures of the Yunnan landscapes and the Alps are other good examples. This point is underlined by the picture on the previous page which involves the 'dubious' technique of sandwiching two slides together, again the ethical stance of a particular technique is not a concern, the end result is my only priority.

The panoramas were composed in Photoshop using five individual shots taken with a 19mm lens and sometimes on a tripod (or in the case of the Tour Ronde a small memorial statue!).

The camera used was a Cannon EOS 500 with lenses from 19mm to 200mm. Polorisers and ND filters were sometimes used as was a tripod and bucket loads of Fuji Velvia 50 asa film. The exceptions were the shots on Bugaboo Spire, when the emergency Kodak 200 asa came into play and also the images of Kilt Rock in Scotland, shot on Ecktapro 25 asa.

The bottom line of my approach to photography and the making of an image can be summed up in three simple steps; i) Take the camera everywhere. ii) Be prepared to use it. iii) Keep an open mind.

For further information with details of how a specific image was captured or produced then please drop me an email - alee@posingproductions.com

ENCORE?

220 degree view, Mark Halsted on the thin holds of the 'Small Smart Wall' (6a) at the Bridestones, Yorkshire, UK. Wiseman Miles Whittaker (left) contemplates the view.

Night climbing on Willan's arete (6a) Widdop, Yorkshire, UK, (15 minute exposure with fill in fash).

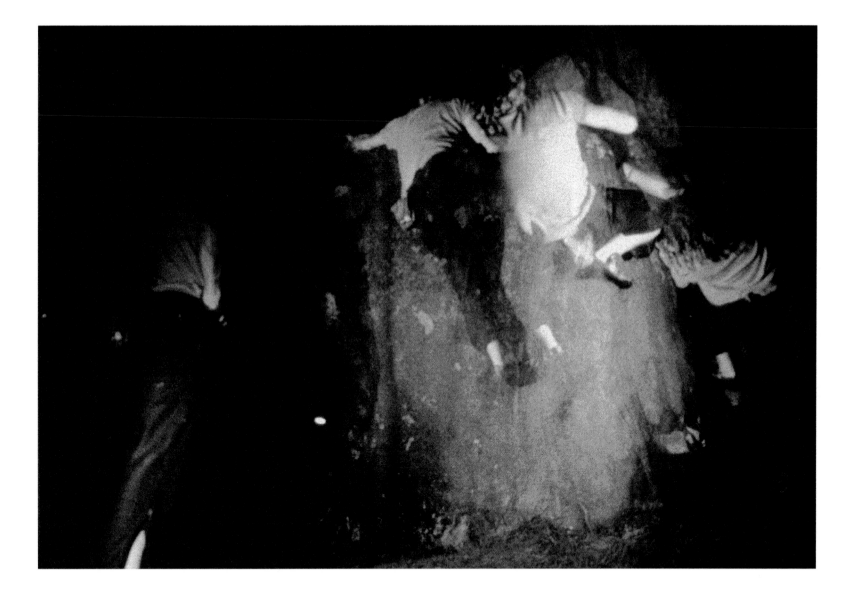

Oliver Drake tackles a 6b traverse in the dark, (long exposure with four shots of the flashgun), Widdop, Yorkshire, UK.

ABOVE - Double exposure of opposing views from the Torino Hut,
Italian side of the Mont Blanc Range, featuring the rock pillar of the Dent du Géant.
RIGHT - Two teams of alpinists scale the NW ridge of Mont Blanc du Tacul.

Dragon/Butterflies feeding on the flora. LEFT - SW Turkey. ABOVE - Stone Forest, Yunnan, China.

Digitally composed image - Swedish climber cut from 'Exasperater' Squamish, BC, Canada.
The foxglove flowers are from the Lancashire Moors, UK.

ABOVE - Digitally composed image, Gatwick airspace and a Bridestones' mantel, UK.
OVERLEAF - Plains lead to the Ogilvie Mountains from the Dempster Highway, Yukon, Canada.

Simon Lv climbs at the 'Copper Door', Yangshuo, China. Two perspectives of the same climb. The Rock is more easily
spotted than the climber in the above picture.